A GLIMPSE OF PARADISE

Barbara Hardwick

ARTHUR H. STOCKWELL LTD
Torrs Park, Ilfracombe, Devon, EX34 8BA
Established 1898
www.ahstockwell.co.uk

British Library Cataloguing-in-Publication Data.
A catalogue record for this book is available
from the British Library.

ISBN 978-0-7223-4188-9
Printed in Great Britain by
Arthur H. Stockwell Ltd
Torrs Park   Ilfracombe
Devon EX34 8BA

Oh, God, please don't desert me.
I want so much to live with Thee;
I want so much to walk Thy way,
To bring us closer every day.
I want to show that through Thy good,
We find at last eternal love.

Why won't you tell me, my dear Lord,
Just what I have to do?
Why won't you put me on the road
That leads direct to you?
Why do I have to love so much
A man who cannot be
The other half of one who gives
Her very soul to Thee?
I could not love Thee more, dear God,
But only when You give
To me the man I love
Will I begin to live.

I wandered in a deep abyss,
To which there was no end.
I felt I had nowhere to turn;
I felt I had no friend.
Then something in my heart did stir,
And to me seemed to say,
"The Lord our God, He is your Friend.
Why don't you kneel and pray?"
And so I came to find the way,
To lead me from despair,
And in my heart I know I'll find
Content when I am there.

My God, if I should try to do
The best I can my whole life through,
Would You grant me just for a time
To be with him whose heart and mine
Are joined in love and by Thy grace
Could live a while in perfect peace?

Dear God, please guide our hearts that we may do
The things that You would want us to.
Be in our minds that we might see with clarity
The truth, and we can come to Thee
With open hearts and know that we may seek
A humble blessing at Thy feet.

Time is a thing that teaches us
So many things, both bad and good.
It teaches us to wait with grace
For the things our hearts give pride of place.
It teaches us to know for sure
If our love is strong enough to endure
The pain and sorrow that it must bring
Before we find a life everlasting.

The hours go by and, more and more,
I know too well I can't ignore
The incredible emptiness in my heart
I always get when we're apart.
I sit and fret and then they come –
The endless questions, one by one.
They fill my heart with doubts and fears,
And while I try to fight the tears
I ask myself, "Why does he care
For someone who is never there,
Who doesn't get a chance to show
Just how and why she loves him so?"
And then my thoughts dance through the years,
And I no longer shed my tears.
My heart swells up with joy and pride,
Because I know that, side by side,
We'll walk the stormy paths of life,
And one day I will be your wife.

Dear God, please forgive my sins;
Please restore my soul;
Please grant to me the gift of love
And make my spirit whole.
Show me Thy way of life;
Let me not drift away.
Please guide someone who longs so much
To walk Thy wondrous way.
Please help me to be kind,
The way I want to be.
My life's no good unless I give
My heart and soul to Thee.

The things around me have not changed;
'Tis I, with opened eyes,
Who sees the things I once passed by.
The beauty of the world is still
The same, but yet I see
Not what they are but what would be
If you and I together looked,
And saw, with opened eyes,
A glimpse of love and paradise.

Where is the love that once was mine?
Where are the hearts that once entwined
To live and love and be as one?
My love, my love, where have you gone?

Where are the hands that once held mine
With tenderness and love divine?
Where are the eyes that spoke the words
We know were there but seldom heard?

Where is the faith, so strong, complete,
That never doubted that we'd meet?
Where is the soul I gave, so free,
For you to keep eternally?

The heartache eased, the sorrow gone –
Once more I know that we are one.
Once more I feel the urgent call
To give my love, my life, my all.

Always and for ever my thoughts are of you.
You are there in my mind in everything I do.
Every moment you're here, deep down in my heart,
And although I am sad because we're apart
There is joy in my heart because I am sure
That whatever may happen our love will endure.

You closed the door then went away,
And my heart cried, "Please make him stay.
Please turn around – it can't be true.
How can I live away from you?"

But you went on with head held high.
I told myself, "Don't cry, don't cry."
Our love must last though we're apart.
Be brave and hide a broken heart.

I am so cold, the house is bare,
I have no home now you're not here.
I see your face the whole day through –
How can I live? What can I do?

Each lonely hour of every day,
How can I live when you're away?
Where is the sun, where is the light?
How can I go to sleep at night?

Where is the magic of each day?
It is not there when you're away.
Where is the eagerness to share?
It cannot be when you're not there.

There is no answer to this ache.
I know for sure my heart will break.
I also know with certainty
I'll love you for eternity.

Please take my love within your heart,
And promise me we'll never part.
Come back to me, my love, please do.
I couldn't live away from you.

The anguish of a tortured soul
Is mine to keep tonight.
My heart cries out for all the things
To which I have no right.
I tell myself, "Please understand.
Please take away the pain."
But this my body won't accept,
And it all starts again.
Forgive me, please. I know you're right.
There's nothing else to do.
Please give me strength to bear the pain
And be as good as you.

The days go by, I smile and chat,
I fill the time with this and that.
I try to push the time along,
But it won't play; it is too strong.
It makes me wait and take the pain
Until I see your face again.

The months go by, turn into years;
The journey long can't halt the tears
Or curb the passion of the soul
For love so strong it cannot go.
The long, long walks, the stolen time –
Will it ever be that you are mine?

One day it changed. Out of the blue,
The time had come to be with you.
The endless years, the waiting done,
The promise kept to live as one.

Now starts the turmoil of the mind.
What happens now? What will we find
When we unlock this other life?
Will love be stronger than the strife?

The work is hard. We must assess
What can be done to start afresh.
We must remember those for whom
This life we live has come too soon.

We try and try and try to make things 'right'.
It never leaves us, day or night.
For there's a price that we must pay,
To be together every day.

The time moves on. We should be three,
But sadly this was not to be.
The months of ecstacy dismissed,
As though, somehow, it didn't exist.
Have I been bad? Did I fail the test?
Did I hear right: "It's for the best"?

The best for whom? Not me, not you.
What else is there we have to do
To purge our souls of this, our 'crime'?
Can this be done? Is there still time?

Can we recover from the day
The Lord took everything away?
What bigger price for what we've done?
We gave our all – we lost our son.

The time moves on with too much speed.
It hardly gives us time to grieve,
But grieve we do in our own way.
It did not leave much time for play.

But through the grieving and the tears,
No one can take away the years
Of undiluted love and joy,
To know we've had our little boy.

There are no words that can convey
What happened to my world that day.
It started off much as before,
Then someone dear walked through the door
To say my life, my love, had gone.
How can I live now I am one?

What thought passed through your marvellous mind,
The precious time before you died?
Did you cry out with your last breath
Before you took the path of death?
Was I with you? Should I have known?
Why did you have to die alone?

The long, long days of deep despair –
How hard it is now you're not here.
The waiting still to hear the door,
Then logic says, "It is no more."
The silent room, the empty chair,
Keeps telling me that you're not there.

But time moves on, you have to cope;
You have to live and pray and hope
That one day we will meet somehow.
I don't know where, I don't know how.
I only know we took the prize –
We found our glimpse of paradise.